Wonders

Wonders

The Best Children's Poems of
Effie Lee Newsome

With illustrations by
Lois Mailou Jones

Compiled by Rudine Sims Bishop

Wordsong
Boyds Mills Press

To the memory of

Effie Lee Newsome and Lois Mailou Jones

with gratitude for their gifts

—R.S.B.

A portion of the royalties from the sale of this book go to support
the Scholarship Fund at Wilberforce University.

Introduction copyright © 1999 by Rudine Sims Bishop
All rights reserved

Published by Wordsong
Boyds Mills Press, Inc.
A Highlights Company
815 Church Street
Honesdale, Pennsylvania 18431
Printed in China

Publisher Cataloging-in-Publication Data

Wonders : the best children's poems of Effie Lee Newsome / compiled
by Rudine Sims Bishop ; illustrated by Lois Mailou Jones—1st ed.
[40]p. : ill. ; cm.
Summary: A collection of poems that originally appeared in Gladiola
Garden and The Crisis.
ISBN 1-56397-788-5 (hc.)
ISBN 1-56397-825-3 (pbk.)
1. Children's poetry, American. 2. American poetry—Afro-American
authors.
[1. Poetry. 2. Afro-Americans.] I. Newsome, Effie Lee. II. Bishop,
Rudine Sims. III. Jones, Lois Mailou, ill. IV. Title.
811.54—dc21 1999 AC CIP
99-62256

First edition, 1999
Book designed by Randall F. Llewellyn
The text of this book is set in Goudy

10 9 8 7 6 5 4 3 2 1 hc
10 9 8 7 6 5 4 3 2 1 pbk

CONTENTS

Introduction

Effie Lee Newsome and Lois Mailou Jones

Mary Effie Lee Newsome was possibly the first African American poet whose body of work consisted primarily of poems for children. Born Mary Effie Lee in Philadelphia in 1885, she was the daughter of an African Methodist Episcopal (A.M.E.) minister. Her father, Benjamin Franklin Lee, was at one time president of Wilberforce University in Ohio, then editor of *The Christian Recorder*, the official A.M.E. church magazine, and later a bishop. Following his calling meant that the family moved a number of times, but in 1896 they settled in Wilberforce.

In 1920 Lee married the Reverend Henry Newsome and soon changed her pen name from Mary Effie Lee to Effie Lee Newsome. She died in 1979, having spent most of the remainder of her life in Wilberforce, where she worked as a librarian at nearby Central State College and at the College of Education at Wilberforce University, the position from which she retired in 1963.

Newsome was well educated, having attended Wilberforce, Oberlin, the Philadelphia Academy of Fine Arts, and the University of Pennsylvania. As a child, she had been an avid reader, and she and her younger sister were also keen observers of the natural world around them. Newsome started writing when she was five. She and her sister also learned to paint and draw when they were children. They submitted some of their writings and sketches to children's magazines, and won a number of prizes.

As an adult, Newsome contributed a number of poems to *The Brownies' Book*, the magazine published in 1920 and 1921 for "the children of the sun" by W.E.B. DuBois, the highly respected rights activist and intellectual leader. Later, from 1925-1929, she wrote a children's column, "The Little Page," for *The Crisis*, the official magazine of the National Association for the Advancement of Colored People (NAACP). The column contained prose sketches, poems, and frequently her own illustrations.

In 1940 the only collection of Newsome's poems, *Gladiola Garden: Poems of Outdoors and Indoors for Second Grade Readers*, was published by Associated Publishers, a company established by Dr. Carter G. Woodson, the highly regarded African American historian and educator. Woodson, founder of the Association for the Study of Negro Life and History, had established the publishing house to make available books that informed Black children of Black achievements and Black history, and promoted pride in themselves and their heritage. Most of the poems in *Wonders* were selected from *Gladiola Garden*, although some had been published first on "The Little Page."

Although she published well over a hundred and fifty poems for children, Newsome's work as a children's poet has been largely forgotten. She was, however, a pioneer, and this collection is an attempt to re-introduce her and the spirit of her work to a new generation of children.

Lois Mailou Jones was an acclaimed and distinguished artist and teacher whose works have been exhibited in many museums and galleries in the United States and abroad. Born in Boston in 1905, Jones attended the High School of Practical Arts, and studied design at the School of the Museum of Fine Arts. She had her first solo show at seventeen on Martha's Vineyard. Early in her career she won awards for her textile designs. In the late 1930s she studied painting in Paris and Italy, and became known for her paintings and drawings as well as her design work.

She taught for a short time at Palmer Memorial Institute in North Carolina, but in 1930 was persuaded to move to the Department of Art at Howard University, where she taught until she retired in 1977. In 1953 she married Louis Vergniaud Pierre-Noâl, a prominent Haitian artist. In addition to continuing to produce her own highly regarded work, Jones became an expert on contemporary Haitian and African art and artists.

Although she was primarily known as a painter and teacher, Jones also had a career as an illustrator. From 1936 through 1965, she illustrated a line of children's books for Associated Publishers, which also produced the *Journal of Negro History* and the *Negro History Bulletin*, a journal suitable for use with school-age children. Lois Mailou Jones understood Carter G. Woodson's intention to reach an audience generally neglected or misrepresented in the children's literature of the time, and provided appealing and finely crafted illustrations for the Negro History Bulletin and for Associated Publishers' children's books, including *Gladiola Garden*.

Unfortunately her fine illustrations for children's books have been largely overlooked by children's literature experts. As is the case with the art in *Gladiola Garden*, however, many of her black-and-white illustrations are treasures that will bring delight to readers young and old alike. Ms. Jones died on June 9, 1998, at the age of 92.

About the Poems

The poems in this book were written more than fifty years ago by a woman who loved all of nature—birds, flowers, trees, wind, rain, snow, insects, animals. Most of Effie Lee Newsome's poems, consequently, are nature poems, reflecting close observation of her natural surroundings in her beloved Wilberforce, Ohio. She could see the wonder in a spider's web or a firefly's light.

She also had a special regard for children and childhood, and some of her poems reflect her own experiences growing up at the turn of the century. She had a knack for being able to remember a child's way of seeing the world. The poems were written in the 1920's and 1930's, a time that is reflected in the illustrations, especially in the old-fashioned look of the clothing, which adds its own special charm. Occasional word choices also reflect an earlier time, but in those cases, meanings are usually clear from the context.

All the children who are pictured in the illustrations are African American. At the time the poems were first published, very few books portrayed African American children at all, and even fewer did so in an attractive and realistic way. These pictures were intended to help to fill a void, and to contradict the popular caricatures that were widely available then. The poems that feature children, however, are not about cultural experiences particular to African Americans, but reflect experiences or emotions common to children across ethnic groups. Since many writers and artists of that era tended to portray African Americans as comical and "different," it was important to writers like Effie Lee Newsome to show that African American children shared such emotions and experiences with children everywhere; that they were in every way "normal," ordinary children.

Newsome's children's poems were usually rhymed and metered, characteristics that invariably appeal to young children. From time to time, she wrote nonsense poems, which have a timeless attraction as well. Two such poems are included in this collection, "Commodore Quiver" and "In All Other Studies They'd Balk." Mainly, however, Effie Lee Newsome's poems offer vivid images of earth and sky and the ordinary plant and animal life we encounter in our everyday world. Lois Mailou Jones's superb illustrations capture the verbal images, enriching and extending them with her own visual interpretations. Together the poems and the illustrations help us to see anew the wonders that surround us in our daily lives, and invite us to take the time to relish the small joys of life.

—Rudine Sims Bishop

Wonders

Wondering

STRANGE

It makes no difference when I wake,
Some little bird has beaten me.
But who calls them before I'm up,
Has always been a mystery.

YOUNG BIRDS' MOUTHS

A nestful of birds' mouths
Is such a surprise.
I peeped in a nest once.
Though there were no cries,
Each bird mouth flew open—
And so did my eyes.

QUOITS

In wintertime I have such fun
When I play quoits with father.
I beat him almost every game.
He never seems to bother.

He looks at mother
And just smiles.
And this is strange to me,
For when he plays with grown-up folks,
He beats them, easily.

Quoits is a game in which a heavy ring is thrown so that it will encircle a peg that has been stuck in the ground. It is similar to horseshoes.

BACK

When I come back from summer camp,
"Why, how you've grown!"
They always say.
I think sometimes they must forget
My tallness when I went away.

OLD COMMODORE QUIVER

Old Commodore Quiver
Went down to the river,
Old Commodore Quiver of Gaul.
He sailed from the shore,
But what he went for
He hadn't a notion at all,
No, he hadn't one notion at all.

Illustration by Effie Lee Newsome

Two Legs,
Four Legs,
Six Legs, Eight

PIGEONS

The pigeons find so much to eat—
I see them pecking in the street.
What is it that they relish so
That they must nibble as they go?

PIGEONS AND PEOPLE

The pigeon's feet are grayish red.
Each time it steps, it jerks its head.
It jerks its head and jerks its feet,
And dodges people on the street.

And people dodge the pigeons too,
Some walking as pigeons do,
Except nobody jerks his head.
The people swing their arms instead.

GEESE

I saw some geese go strutting by
With heads and necks held very high.
I saw six geese upon the lawn,
And each had boots of orange on.

IN ALL OTHER STUDIES THEY'D BALK

"Proff" Pea-green, the parrot,
Kept school in a garret
To teach other parrots to talk.
The way they learned mocking
Was something quite shocking.
In all other studies they'd balk.

A Turtle with a Tiny Head

A turtle with a tiny head
And little streaks of Chinese red
Came trotting gaily to the lawn
One summer day at early dawn.

I tapped him lightly with a stick.
He drew his head and legs in, quick.
Strange turtle with your streaks of red.
And folding legs and hiding head!

from TWO FIREFLY SONGS

The firefly
Goes flashing by,
A lemon-golden spark,
A dancing Rhinestone in the sky,
A jewel in the dark.

from FIREFLY LIGHTS

At dull blue dusk
I've often seen
Bright fireflies flash their silver green.

THE WALK

A ladybird went for a walk
Up in a great French horn,
And wandered round and round and round
Until her feet were worn.

THE GOLDEN GARDEN SPIDER

The golden garden spider
Has grasshoppers for lunch—
At least they hang beside her—
I've never seen her munch.
And yet they swing there every day,
And always in a different way.

Sometimes I glance at her at dawn,
But seldom find her food all gone.
It isn't hard to tell you why—
She traps grasshoppers passing by,
Then wraps them in her web all day.
When their long legs get caught they stay,
And kicking don't do any good—
Somehow, sometimes—I wish it would.

Flowers and Trees

Tulip Umbrellas

Tulip umbrellas, gold and red,
Close tight when there's a shower.
That's just when people lift theirs up,—
It's different with a flower.

VIOLETS

The sunflowers wear great gold farm hats,
The poppies red silk hoods.
But violets wear their bowed heads bare
On highways or in woods.

CHANGE

There's been the strangest kind of change
Since autumn came into the woods.
The mountain maples' summer hats
Have turned to bright red riding hoods.

WRITING

Bare boughs look like black pencil marks
On great white books of snow.
But what the writing really is,
No one on earth would know,
With X's, V's, and W's,
And loops and curves and curlicues.

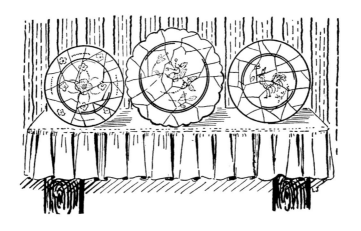

WINTER SHADOWS

Night shadows of the trees streak snow
With little twisted tracks
Like markings on grandmother's plates,
The old ones that have cracks.

Weather and Sky

WINTER MORNING

Who wrapped the moon
Like candy balls
In waxy tissue paper fold?
I saw it shortly after dawn
When all the pale south sky looked cold.

SNOW PRINTS

Along the paths my overshoes
Make little pits in twos and twos.
But often on that very day
The sunshine melts them all away.

It seems a funny kind of waste,
These footprints getting all erased.
It takes a very icy day
To ever make them really stay.

THE SNOW

The snow's a courteous visitor.
It brings its blankets as it comes,
And goes to bed right on the ground.
It never snores or makes a sound.

BEFORE THE WHITE ROUND MOON

Before the white round moon,
The fat clouds tumble up and down,
Each like a padded, puffy clown.
That couldn't quite jump through.

FLAKES AND DROPS

The snow comes down in little flakes
And rain in little drops.
The water helps to swell the lakes
And goes to moisten crops.